Image & Likeness

UNVEILING THE TWENTY-SEVEN DIMENSIONS OF MAN...
Condensed Version

Melinda Lis Solomon Badhai

Scripture taken from the King James Version of the Bible.

WestBow Press books may be ordered through booksellers or by contacting:

WestBow Press
A Division of Thomas Nelson
1663 Liberty Drive
Bloomington, IN 47403
www.westbowpress.com
1-(866) 928-1240

ISBN: 978-1-4497-1217-4 (sc)
ISBN: 978-1-4497-1218-1 (e)

Library of Congress Control Number: 2011922281

Printed in the United States of America

WestBow Press rev. date: 5/5/2011

UNVEILING THE TWENTY-SEVEN DIMENSIONS OF MAN...

INTRODUCTION

"What is man, that You should exalt him, that You should set Your heart on him...What is man that You are mindful of him, and the son of man that You visit him? For You have made him a little lower than the angels, And you have crowned him with glory and honor." Job 7:17; Psalm 8:4,5

According to scripture man was made in the image and likeness of God and for this reason he is in portion the fixation of the physical and material world and has from birth gained the attentive care of God as Father and Creator. God relates with this particular portion of creation as Father and Creator in both the physical and invisible realm. While God is the creator of all things He does not Father all creatures. He fathers redeemed man; fathering not a portion of man but the whole man, spirit, soul and body because the redeemed man is established in Christ Jesus **(Luke 3:38; Hebrews 12:9; Numbers 16:22)**. Man is the expression of an infinite God in a finite world. Out of all of God's creation, man was created special.

Man is the most complex and the most distinct of all God's creation (he is the image and likeness of God according to **Genesis 1:26, 27**). Man is a multi-dimensional being in a physical body capable of interacting with both physical and immaterial (spiritual) spheres. The capacity to interact with both physical and spiritual spheres was placed in the nature of man's being according to *Genesis 2:7: " And the Lord God formed man of the dust of the ground and breathed into his nostrils; and man became a living soul"*. Man's formation from the dust of the earth permitted him access and interaction with his physical environment, while the breath of God (spirit) in him permitted him access to his spiritual environment. Man is the most superior being on the face of the earth and outside of God Himself; man is the most influential being operating in the spirit realm. Man was formed in a manner superior to the rest of creation, being fashioned as a result of a delicate mediate creation unlike the rest of creation process which was brought forth immediately without process **(compare Genesis 1:12,24 vs. Genesis 2:7 Zechariah 12:1).** Unlike other living creatures, including the angelic, man has a dichotomous nature, being natural in his body but supernatural in his spirit and soul. Samuel Harris states in The Philosophical Basis of Theism:

> *"Man, though implicated in nature through his bodily organization, is in his personality supernatural; the brute [animal] is wholly submerged in nature.... Man is like a ship in the sea- in it, yet above it- guiding his course, by observing the heavens, even against wind and current. A brute [animal] has no such power; it is in nature like a balloon, wholly immersed in air, and driven about by its currents with no power steering."*

In this statement Harris shows the distinction between humans and animals as well as the distinction between man's physical nature and his spiritual nature. Because man was created in the image and likeness of God, in the earth he is the representation of God to all of creation. God designed man with complexity, depth and dimension *like* Himself and in this, man is unique from all other creations including the angelic. Again man is a multidimensional being for which physical and spiritual spheres serve as active environments.

THE REALITY AND DIVERSITY OF SPHERES

Because man is made up of physical (natural) and spiritual (supernatural) parts, he operates in physical and spiritual spheres, daily interacting in visible and invisible environments. Each sphere is a reality, not a mystical substance, but an actual place of existence in which a form of life operates. While there are many spheres there are three predominant spheres of existence: Heaven, Earth and Hell, which are all destinational places as well as experiential realities. While there are several supernatural spheres Genesis 1 shows us that God only created one natural sphere of creation (one physical world incorporating earth, solar systems, galaxies and the universe). While man is stationed in earth he engages and interacts with heaven and/ or hell as experiential realities. As indicated in the following diagram, the spheres of heaven and the spheres of hell do not directly engage one another. Rather, both spheres impose their influence upon man and subsequently on earth. Man as the crown of creation retains the authority to choose which influence he will allow to govern him and influence his physical environment (Genesis 1:26,28).

Depending upon which sphere man has engaged the most and attained the most inner likeness to, will determine which supernatural sphere he will encounter as a destinational place after death (a.1). Those who are heaven bound are assured of this in earth because they carry within them the substance of heaven (the Holy Ghost (Colossians 1:27)) and after death will not be attracted to a contrary place.

Those who have rebelled against God either passively or aggressively can be assured their spot in hell for they carry within themselves the nature of hell (rebellion) and their spirit man will be attracted to the environment to which they have the most likeness **(Revelation 20:10, 12-15)**. This is the spiritual law of attraction.

* Destinational Heaven Rev 19:11 Experiential Heaven Eph1:3, 2:6
* Destinational Hell Lu 16:23 Experiential Hell Psalm 116:3

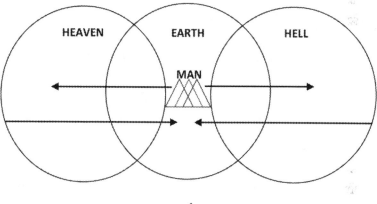

a.1

Sir Issac Newton, the physicist, discovered that there was a natural law that existed within all creation that attracted like substances to one another. In his work *Philosophiae Naturalis Principia Mathematica,* published on July 5, 1687 he expounds on his discovery which he entitles the *law of universal gravitation (diagram a.2)*. This law states that every massive particle in the universe attracts every other massive particle with a force which is directly proportional to the product of their masses and inversely proportional to the square of the distance between them. In other words, everything in natural creation has a natural attraction to gravitate toward objects of like substance and force. This natural law holds true for all physical creation.

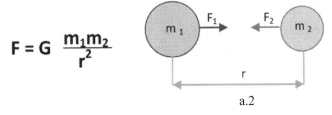

$$F = G \, \frac{m_1 m_2}{r^2}$$

a.2

Nevertheless there is a spiritual law of attraction which exists between man and his supernatural environments which affects not only the spirit and soul of man but also inadvertently effects his physical environment. Whatever force we gravitate to spiritually will gravitate toward us. Whatever we draw closer to we will become of like substance to. As we are recognized amongst our relatives in the earth realm for bearing resemblance and similar physical attributes, likewise we are categorized as to which supernatural sphere we belong to based on the resemblance of the image of our spiritual man. The interactions we have with both our physical and spiritual environments form our identity in over twenty-seven dimensions of our being.

UNVEILING THE
DIMENSIONS OF MAN

A dimension of man can be defined as a measurable plane or place of capacity designed to facilitate a specific expression of life. Man was created triune in essence, being composed of a body (soma), soul (psyche) and a spirit (pneuma) which operate unified with one another forming one person (Genesis 2:7). These parts are not isolated from one another (a.3) or a functioning man would be impossible, neither is one part larger than the other (a.4) or man would be unbalanced. Rather, they are unified yet distinct and possessing many dimensions between them (a.5) (1 Thessalonians 5:23).

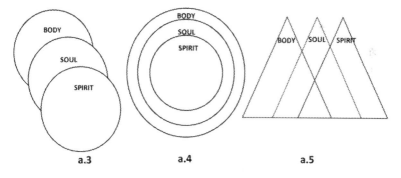

a.3   a.4   a.5

Diagram a.3 represents a false belief that the trinity of man operates uninfluenced by one another and autonomous in nature. If this were true the world would be filled with lifeless corpses, disembodies souls, and life surging mists of spirits floating through the atmosphere painting a perfect picture of a sci-fi movie. As foolish as this theory sounds it is a good depiction of the belief of most people (saved and sinner alike). Individuals with this philosophy believe that the sins they commit with their body do not influence their spirit and cannot hinder the destination of their soul. This false belief resembles that of agnosticism, an erroneous belief system that arose during early Christianity. This religion set many early Christians astray, reinforcing the idealism of a carnal Christian who could drink, fornicate, and curse without endangering the salvation of his soul. Early church fathers fought diligently against similar teachings because they knew that it would lead to the condemnation of the whole man. This theory is easily refuted by the fact that sin does not originate in the body but in the soul where it is conceived. The Apostle Paul in **1 Corinthians 6:9-10** spoke out against such theories, emphasizing that those that practiced bodily lawlessness violated the whole man and would not inherit the kingdom of God.

Diagram a.4 represents the false belief that the trinity of man is naturally imbalanced. It supposes that man's greater portion is his body which encapsulates his soul, which houses his spirit which is the lesser (but more potent) portion of his nature. Much like the theory of diagram a.2 it also supposes that the spirit has no connection to the body. This too is false. This falsity would then equally suppose that God created man to have a greater interaction with his physical environment than he ever could with supernatural environment. This would also mean that when man dies and puts off his flesh the greater portion of him has died. All of which is false. If this were the case the spirit man would have no power to subdue the will of the flesh and no perspicacity to attain that which is spiritual. If this were our condition a relationship with God who is Spirit would be impossible because of the restraints of our natural body.

However, the illustration of diagram a.5 shows us how man is truly united. The body, soul, and spirit are distinct, intertwined and proportionately equal, operating simultaneously and harmoniously. **1 Thessalonians 5:23** expresses that the triune parts of man are to be equally saved and preserved and sanctified by the acceptance of the complete work of Christ. Within the balanced union of man's triune nature, the dimensions of man are established. Under the realization of our structure and Christ's desire to rule over the whole man, we can begin to allow the grace, glory and fellowship of Christ to reign in every dimension of our being.

There are over twenty-seven dimensions of man. These dimensions facilitate expressions of life within and emanating from man. There are over twenty-seven corridors and expressions of our life in which our Lord and Savior Jesus Christ desires to fellowship and unite with us personally. Over twenty-seven dimensions of man that are desperately in need of co-crucifixion and union with Christ. You may be saved, but we must daily examine ourselves to ensure that we are not denying ourselves the opportunity to invite all of God into all of us and have Holy Communion with Him **(1 Corinthians 11:28)**. It is time to enter into a deeper relationship with the God whom we love. Before God can reveal to us the deeper things in Him we must have a realization of the deep things in us. Ask the Lord **"Father please reveal my deeper identity to me so You can truly be glorified through me as I become truly transparent through You. Amen."**

WHAT IS MAN?

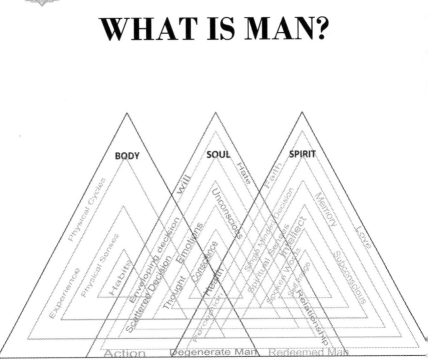

Man is the image and likeness of God; a multidimensional being composed of a triune nature (body, soul, and spirit) and a dichotomous nature (being both natural and supernatural). Man is a living creature capable of engaging both physical and immaterial spheres. Man is the only creation which can relate to God as creature to Creator and as child to Father. Man is the image and likeness of an infinite God in a finite world and in this man is in his simplest definition a masterpiece of God.

CHAPTER ONE
THE DIMENSION OF THE WILL

The will provides a great distinction between man and beast, and distinguishes the resemblance between man and God. The dimension of the will consists of volition, motivation, aspiration, desire and ambition. Each is a distinct element with similar functions which impact the overall will of man. The will is the driving force of man's personality and affects every faculty of man's life determining things like choice, tolerance and intensity of pursuit.

The will of man is a free variable, instituted by God so that man would have freedom in his relationship with God, relating to God with the freedom of a son to a father unlike the restrains and demanded obedience of a dog relating to his master. The original state of the will was free in innocent obedience; a will that was directed only in one way, towards God. This was the will of Adam and Eve prior to the fall. The will of the redeemed man is restored to this state once he commits his life to full obedience to God. This is the only time that man's will mirrors that of the perfect will of God, when he chooses to direct his volition, motivation, aspiration, desire and ambition toward the Lord, submitting to and obeying the will of God by choice.

The dimension of the will in the unredeemed man remains degenerative in the fallen nature of Adam. The first act of volition was performed in **Genesis 3:6** establishing the will of man in sin **(Genesis 6:5 Ecclesiastes 9:3)**, for this reason the dimension of the will is continuously in need of repentance and transformation by the Holy Spirit **(Romans 7:18-20;**

Philippians 2:13). Without such the will of man becomes his own poison driving him to his own death by godless aspirations, motivations, and desires. Like Adam and Eve most sinners do not continue to sin willfully desiring to assault the nature of their soul. Neither do they sin willfully desiring to do evil in the sight of God. Rather they sin because their perception has persuaded them that "they will not surely die" that the way that they have chosen is justified in their eyes. Eve's warped perception first deceived her will and her desires. This deception caused her will to comply with a sin that her conscience mind justified and her perception submitted to. Most people in the earth are not sinning because they want to go to hell but because there will continues to perform unconscious patterns of sin. These patterns of sins can only be broken by a conscience, willful choice to receive Jesus Christ as Lord and Savior. This willful choice allows man to receive a reconciliation and redemption from his sins that he could not achieve by any other means **(Romans 10:13)**. By choosing Christ we willfully allow God to come into our personal life and rectify the process of sin working in our souls and remove the penalty of death from over our lives. Could God sovereignly choose to bypass the will of mankind and redeem each soul without their personal consent? Yes, but no.

God is governed by Himself and will not lie or change the rules in the middle of the game **(Number 23:19)**. If He gave man free will then he wants man to use it to glorify Him **(Deuteronomy 30:19)**. If God were to forcefully subdue the will of man His image would be tarnished. All other earthly creatures respond to God by nature of obedience. However, these creatures are no benefactors to salvation which can only be received by free will. By choice we enter the new covenant with God not by force. The will is the door to salvation (Revelation 3:20). While man is saved through faith in his personal acceptance of Jesus Christ, faith cannot operate until the will makes a choice to be saved. The will must be turned over to God in order for the whole man to be saved.

The free will of man has always been necessary in order to establish a covenant with man. In the Old Testament we see that God speaks to Noah, Abraham and concerning Isaac, establishing a covenant with each (Genesis 6:18; 17:7,21). Each covenant was established with each patriarch as he freely agreed with God. Further along in scripture the Lord ordains the holy custom of the free will offering in Israel. This custom was a sign between God and man, signifying man's personal agreement with the covenant that God established with him (Deuteronomy 23:23, Numbers 29:39, Leviticus 22:18,21,23). This symbolic offering represents the sacrifice of freely submitting one's will in order to be in agreement with God. Laying aside internal discord, doubt, opinions and biases and fully accepting what God has said despite experience and/or feelings. By this the free will not only seals the covenant with God but also continues to activate it in our lives. The fullness of God's Word (CHRIST) is our New Covenant (Psalm 119:108a vs. Romans 10:13). His nature is sealed in us as we receive His words; and each word is activated in our life by our free will to submit to the Word of God and operate by faith in what our New Covenant says.

The will motivates the eternal motions of man. It is our willful action and our willful choice of being (choosing the spiritual state of death or life, sin or salvation) that will put a momentum behind our attraction to heaven or hell.

The will of today will pay for the choice of tomorrow. The will of man propels him through life. The predicament or state of being that we find ourselves in almost always matches the state of our will. Our will will always attract us to an eternal place which best manifests the image of what we are on the inside. The man who goes to hell chooses hell while in earth and after death finds the essence of his being being most attracted to a sphere of hell then to a sphere of heaven. In fact though he is now eternally tortured by his sin, he is more comfortable there than he would be in heaven because he is in the environment that matches his being. We can see this best exampled by the story of the rich man and Lazarus as illustrated by Jesus Christ in **Luke 16:19-26**:

> [19]*There was a certain rich man, which was clothed in purple and fine linen, and fared sumptuously every day:* [20]*And there was a certain beggar named Lazarus, which was laid at his gate, full of sores,* [21]*And desiring to be fed with the crumbs which fell from the rich man's table: moreover the dogs came and licked his sores.* [22]*And it came to pass, that the beggar died, and was carried by the angels into Abraham's bosom: the rich man also died, and was buried;* [23]*And in hell he lift up his eyes, being in torments, and seeth Abraham afar off, and Lazarus in his bosom.* [24]*And he cried and said, Father Abraham, have mercy on me, and send Lazarus, that he may dip the tip of his finger in water, and cool my tongue; for I am tormented in this flame.* [25]*But Abraham said, Son, remember that thou in thy lifetime receivedst thy good things, and likewise Lazarus evil things: but now he is comforted, and thou art tormented.* [26]*And beside all this, between us and you there is a great gulf fixed: so that they which would pass from hence to you cannot;*

*neither can they pass to us, that would come from
thence.*

Through this scripture we note the destination of two men.
One man is in a sphere of hell (Sheol and/or Hades) and one
in a sphere of heaven. We may also take notice of their will
prior to eternal destination, one being described as a wealthy
man overtaken with materialism and pride, while the other
was humbled by life desiring nothing grandiose but only the
bare essentials of life. The destination of these two men
further reveals the image of their inner nature. However the
stranger thing to notice is that nowhere in the passage does
the rich man's dialogue indicate him being surprised about
finding himself in Sheol. Nowhere in scripture does he
express a desire to be removed from that place and be placed
in heaven. Rather he cries out to experience a form of relief
while continuing to exist in his hell. Likewise are the people
of today who have no desire to be saved in earth and are
most comfortable in their sins and in their current hellish
state. In hell they will not desire heaven; they will only
desire relief from the fire of their consequences. We may
also note that while the rich man's dialogue is recorded,
there is no dialogue provided for Lazarus. Lazarus in his
eternal state and in his eternal destination is finally fully
content and has no need to express a petition or a plea.

Lastly we note what Abraham describes as a gulf
fixed between the eternal destinations of heaven and hell.
This gulf is a vast disconnection from the two eternal states
emphasizing the drastic contrast between the natures of both
spheres. Likewise this gulf fixed existed between the will
and the inner nature of these two men emphasizing the
contrast of their natures in life and after death.

In the end, our inner nature will determine our eternal destination. **2 Peter 3:9** shows us that the Lord does not will that any man should perish. It is the deceived and corrupt will of man that causes him to repel himself from the Lord and be attracted toward hell. Though the Lord has good will towards all men He allotted man to have a will for himself. In light of the grace of God the fact still remains that it is our will which drives us to make choices; it is our choices which allow us to attract and receive from heaven or hell; it is what we choose to receive that defines and develops the image of our inner nature; it is the image of our inner nature which will determine our eternal destination.

CHAPTER TWO
THE DIMENSION OF SINGLE-MINDED DECISION

The dimension of single-minded decision is not inherent in the nature of fallen man rather it is developed in the stability of a Christian, in which the soul is settled and slowed (by the Holy Ghost) to receive and interpret one stimulus and produce one answer **(Matthew 5:37)**. This dimension is only developed by an individual who has been disciplined to hear the singular voice of God. Afterwards this dimension becomes applicable to other areas of life.

Single-minded decision is the dimension that produces clarity and soundness in the whole man. This dimension requires clear agreement with the Lord in order for us to develop into a mature Christian. Single-minded decision is an indication of a deeper transformation of the mind, as we take on the image of Christ in our thought process. It is a deeper level of **Philippians 2:5**. When this dimension has been developed we can seek God for His will and purpose, receive an answer and execute the action of His instruction without wavering. Single-minded decision not only excludes the stimuli of other outward voices, opinions and situations, but it also excludes any internal opinions, motivations, rationale and doubts that would stand in conflict with the voice of God. The single stimulus received in this dimension is the voice of God, entailing His will (instruction), His feelings, and His purposes. This single stimulus can be received first through the Word of God, as well as through prophecy, divine inspiration, godly council, prayer, open visions, dreams, interpretation of tongues, the preached word, the taught word, signs, wonders and divine experience. In order for the dimension of single-minded decision to function the voice of God must be received correctly. The interpretation of God's Word must be unhampered with the other stimuli previously discussed. When His Word is received freely, interpreted correctly, and left unmixed with inferior stimuli, man is then able to operate in single-minded decision and walk in the Spirit according to **Galatians 5:16 (see also Psalm 1:1).**

It is important to know that the dimension of single-minded decision is not developed as a result of some kind of unattainable human perfection. However it is developed within the being of a perfect (mature) Christian who receives the grace of God freely, and has become disciplined in his submission to God. At some point in our Christian walk with God, His voice must become the greater influence guiding our life. If you find it difficult to hear the voice of God, maybe it is time for you to reevaluate what other influences are speaking to you. The voice of God is rarely found speaking amongst other mumbling thoughts, babbling idols or grumbling opinions. His voice is most easily discerned through the Word of God and through an intimate prayer life.

CHAPTER THREE
THE DIMENSION OF ENVELOPING DECISION

The dimension of enveloping decision receives and interprets multiple stimuli to conclude one answer. An individual who operates in this dimension relies on information gathered from many sources to conclude one answer. Because this dimension incorporates many opinions, facts and stimuli it often concludes the wrong answer. It is important to note in light of this that God does not speak amongst the chorus on many voices and opinions. He is too sovereign to contest against inferior opinions (1 Corinthians 3:19-20). He leaves it to our discretion whether we will receive His omniscient wisdom concerning a matter or if we choose to adhere to wisdom from below (James 3:15,17; exp 1 Samuel 27: 3-27). Any wisdom that is not from above is from below because there is no wisdom that originates in man. Man can only receive wisdom. It is important for us to surround ourselves with Godly council (Psalm 1:1) and to be led by the Spirit (Romans 8:14) so that the dimension of single-minded decision can be developed.

It is easy for an individual operating in the dimension of enveloping decision to become prideful. Individuals who operate heavily in this dimension usually operate in intellectual pride. They esteem themselves in being able to take in and interpret large amounts of information, dissect a multiplicity of variables and produce the most logical and apparent answer. Man is a logical being and logic belongs to man because man has limits. However God does not operate based upon logic He operates based on being a limitless God and for this reason often times the answers He provides us with are illogical and work beyond intellect. God always provides the correct answer for every question and situation because His wisdom for human circumstance does not stem from fact or cause and effect. The wisdom and answers of God stem from the attribute of His omniscience. This is why we desperately need the opinion of the Holy Spirit active in our lives. We need to discern what the Holy Spirit is saying within us.

This dimension while still decisive can be dangerous because a great majority of what is taken in is unnecessary and if not discarded can produce clutter in the soul. A cluttered soul becomes sluggish, slothful, stressed and unreceptive to the Holy Spirit. Excess stimuli weigh down the mind because so much energy must be exerted to process these great quantities of information. An exhausted mind becomes vulnerable to demonic projections because it is no longer girded by truth. Truth is not merely the Word of God it is the sovereign opinion and the Spirit expressed through the Word of God.

What we allow in stays in until we remove it. We must pray daily and ask God to help us discard intellectual and emotional trash from our mind and upload the truth of His Word through His Spirit.

CHAPTER FOUR
THE DIMENSION OF SCATTERED DECISION

The dimension of scattered decision is the where every unbeliever and every unbelieving believer operate from because they have not yet come to believe in THE WAY, THE TRUTH, and THE LIFE (**John 14:6**). An individual operating without Christ has no true stability in himself. This individual's decisions are scattered because he is un-unified within himself (there is no agreement and unity between his spirit, soul and body). When man lacks unity with God it is impossible for him to be unified within himself. In this dimension various and random stimuli are received and interpreted to produce multiple incomplete decisions; producing confusion. Scattered decision is the kind of thought process that operates within an unwise man (**James 1:5-8, 4:8**). A person that continues to engage life while developing defective conclusions will remain unfulfilled. Their life will constantly be moved by circumstance and tangled by a diversity of opinions. They will lack the ability to produce resolution in the areas of relationship, purpose and internal satisfaction. Scattered decision will always result in an incomplete existence that lacks direction.

The realm of scattered decision is one that decomposes the other dimensions of man, removing soundness of mind and degrading the very principals of sanity. The human mind was not created to wrestle with the opinions of others and a diversity of misguiding stimuli, so we are instructed to cast down such things in **2 Corinthians 10:5**. Like Adam and Eve in the Garden of Eden, a man who surrenders to misguiding external influences will always find himself circum to a fallen state to which the only solution is to adhere to the voice of God for reconciliation **(Genesis 3)**. The dimension of scattered decision can be likened unto what scripture describes to be a double-minded man. The only solution to a double-minded existence is to adhere to the sovereign soundness of the mind of God expressed through His holy scriptures.

To be double-minded in the original context referred to someone who had the appearance of two souls at conflict within him. This individual forms a secondary identity within himself based upon other opinions he has internalized. This identity remains in conflict with his soul and is constantly promoting ideas contrary to what a sober mind would think. This person now has the appearance of two souls because his statements and actions are contradictory and never consistent with one train of thought.

CHAPTER FIVE
THE DIMENSION OF THOUGHT

Thought is the immaterial activity of the mind. When concentrated upon thought can birth physical activity which in turn produces material manifestations. The dimension of thought also expresses an elaborate and lively part of man which may never be expressed outside of the boundaries of the mind. For this reason whatever greatly posses the thoughts of man will be manifested in an equivalent magnitude. The thoughts of man, like God's thoughts, are shielded from the public view of the angelic and can only be seen by God (Luke 9:47; 1Corinthians 3:20). While thought is a concealed dimension of man's spiritual nature, it is an evident factor behind our conscience and unconscious behaviors. In spiritual spheres thought speech and action are equivalent. While angels, demons and humans cannot read our thoughts they can perceive and assume our thinking patterns based upon our actions.

Thought is an elaborate dimension which is continuously active and continuously communicating to God and to others through our actions. Because this dimension is continuously active receiving, interpreting and producing information, it is important to be ever mindful to guard our thoughts from demonic and interpersonal projections. Misguided thoughts stem from one of two places: demonic projections generated in the atmosphere around us or interpersonal projections rising up within us without the counsel of the Holy Spirit. Thoughts can be planted by suggestions and harvested by circumstances, conversations or other external triggers. We must wear the helmet of salvation at all times **(Ephesians 6:17)** in order to guard our minds from these ungodly invasion, because whatever we allow to be conceived in thought will be birthed in action.

Thought produces action according to **Philippians 4:8,9.** Thought is the womb of possibility and the place from which all manmade creations derive. The thoughts of man made manifest has produced great monuments such as the Great Wall of China, the Panama Canal and the Statue of Liberty. The thoughts of man made manifest determined great philosophies and sciences. Nevertheless these thoughts and the fruits thereof shrivel in comparison to the immensity of the thought of God.

It was the thoughts of God that planned the architecture of the universe placing each galaxy on a balanced ellipsis and setting each planet in its orbit. And it is the omniscient thoughts of God that gazes on the past and future and counts them all as present. For this reason the Lord looks upon the deepest contemplations of man and the greatest minds to every walk the earth and declares, *"...My thoughts are not your thoughts..."* in **Isaiah 55:8.** The thoughts of God are established forever and will not pass away. However, the thoughts of man are as fleeting as his existence. Unless the thoughts of God are expressed through us, our unguided thoughts will accomplish very little **(Psalm 94:11).**

CHAPTER SIX
THE DIMENSION OF INTELLECT

The dimension of the intellect is not defined by intelligence but defined by ones capacity to receive and be taught. The highest contemplation of man is not in calculus, philosophy or physics. The greatest exercise of man's intellect is in theology, where the mind gazes upon a contemplation (God) that he will never fully comprehend and cannot master. Here, in drawing closer to God the whole man is enriched, as he receives what he rightfully should not be able to contain. This is the beginning of knowledge (**Proverbs 1:7**). Our ability to receive from God in our intellect is an act of grace because technically the frailty of man is unable to endure the contemplation of God without being destroyed by His awesomeness. The 12 Apostles of the Lamb were noted for having a great grace upon them, (**Acts 4:33**) which was necessary for them to exercise the power of God in miracles and exegete sound doctrine to the church. This grace to receive from God in our intellect is not given to those who strive vainly to receive religious intelligence. Rather it is given to those who surrender their loft reasoning and humble themselves for the sake of desiring to know God (**James 4:6**).

Within the dimension of intellect elements like creativity, studiousness and development are first initiated or fractured. Learning the wrong things can stunt and hinder the development of the imagination and creativity. Negative learning patterns, like rebellion against instruction, can hinder the intellectual growth of an individual, and though they may appear smart, the bible defines this kind of person as a fool **(Proverbs 1:7)**. The intellect of man must be transfigured by receiving the Word of God humbly. The intellect of man is transfigured after the heart has humbled itself and after the perception has surrendered its opinions.

Man is not ranked as the most intelligible being amongst all of God's creation. In fact, angelic beings far surpass man in intelligence in both their capacity to receive and by experience. Their age alone surpasses that of the oldest man to walk the earth giving them the advantage of experience. The only time when the intelligence of man can equate the intelligence of the angelic is when our mind is illuminated by the divine revelation of the Lord. The intelligence of engineers and philosophers are esteemed highly in the earth, but the omniscient intelligence of one Carpenter has by far superseded the intelligence of both men and angels. Jesus Christ was the only human who has every walked the face of the earth with perfect intellect.

CHAPTER SEVEN
THE DIMENSION OF EMOTIONS

Emotion is a necessary dimension of man but is often an over active component. Emotion is one of the most sensitive dimensions of man. It is easily touched and accessible to experiences and thoughts. Even the slightest imbalance in man can send this dimension haywire on emotional tangents. This dimension is still governed by the will of man. In this dimension the predominant disposition of one's personality is established. Despite popular belief God is not coming in to drastically alter our emotional state against our will. He will not wrestle with negative attitudes, depression or any other degeneracy that we've chosen to adopt in our emotions. Rather He makes provision for us to maintain healthy emotions by adhering to the following scriptures and living by the virtues presented in them:

Self Control- **Galatians 5:23; 2Peter 1:6**

Joy- **Isaiah 61:3; Romans 15:13**

*Laughter-***Proverbs 17:22**

*Praise-***Isaiah 61:3; Psalm 34:1; 147:1**

*Trust in the Lord-***Psalm 37:3; Proverbs 3:5**

Emotions were not designed to torment man but to beautify his soul. Our ability to express ourselves through emotions is a part of our humanity. Our ability to add emotion to our memories, experiences and thoughts shows that God intended for man to be emotionally connected to both his spiritual and physical experiential environments. We are not to pray to God and ask Him to remove our emotions rather we are to ask God to assist us in using the tools provided in scripture to structure our emotional life.

Emotions are not supposed to be absent from our personal, social or ministerial lives as Christians. Rather, our emotions are to be used as a vehicle to convey the heart of God through His message to man (exp. The Prophet Jeremiah).

If the dimension of emotions is injured it may result in apathy. An apathetic Christian is no good to himself or to the kingdom of God because he lacks the ability to touch the heart of God in prayer or intercession **(Hebrews 14:15)**. This kind of an individual cannot feel the burden of those around him and therefore will also fail to intercede for them. Christ Himself took on the state of man, suffered and died that he may be acquainted with our joys and our cries when we call upon Him. An apathetic Christian lacks an essential element of Christ's character, empathy. Usually individuals in this state find themselves lost in pride. They have mistaken the grace of God that delivered them, to be an excuse to boast in their deliverance, but never dirty their fingers to bring grace to someone else who is in need of the same deliverance. This individual also fails to have a soft heart toward God and therefore cannot receive the love and grace of the heart of God that He expresses to us in intimate prayer. God desires to not only convey His revelation and knowledge through us but to convey His heart to others and establish His love in us.

CHAPTER EIGHT
THE DIMENSION OF PERCEPTION

The dimension of perception is a culmination of personality and experience but often makes misguided internal judgments of the external world **(Genesis 3:6 Proverbs 16:2, 21:2; Matthew 7:2-4)**. Perception is our internal eye. It has shades of vision that are tinted by intrinsic components such as biases, beliefs and values and external observations such as social influences, relationships and time. Much like our natural eye our perception takes in external stimuli translates it in broad terms based on our internal values and then focuses the meaning of what we've perceived based on the context of the presented stimuli.

Our perception is the part of us that puts our personal definition of right and wrong into perspective for every situation. The problem with every man's perception is that it often determines standards of right and wrong (good and evil) which do not line us with God's truth of what is right and what is wrong **(Proverbs 14:12 16:25)**. This internal sight must be given over to God so we can be led by the Spirit to walk by faith and not by sight **(2Corinthian 5:7)**.

Discernment, while very similar to perception, is a faith based form of sight (not a fleshly/natural form of sight) which can only operate when unrestricted by our predetermined perceptions. Faith in itself is not a blind hoping, rather it is an assured vision and manifestation solely based on our belief in what God can and will do. While natural perception has a tendency to steer the soul in the wrong direction faith has a 100% chance of guiding us in the way that will please God **(Hebrews 11:6)**. **1Corithians 2:9** shows us that natural perception does not have the ability to perceive the works of God. In order to perceive or receive prophetically from God we must deny natural perception and enable our faith to see for us **(Jeremiah 1:11-19)**.

Perception is a powerful dimension of man because it guides us in our judgments, receptivity and decisions. The dimension of perception is also a remarkable component of man that connects him with his environment and in itself is not evil. However if this dimension is not surrendered to God it can become a tool of the enemy to work out wicked things like racism, prejudice, fear and displaced hatred in the soul of man.

CHAPTER NINE
THE DIMENSION OF FAITH

The dimension of faith sets order to the other twenty-six dimensions of man. The dimension of faith working in us has the ability to change our perception, increase our health, heighten our spiritual senses and align our internal man in preparation to perform outward works. Faith is the dimension within the spirit that receives life and distributes it to the rest of man saving the whole man (Mark 10:52; Acts 15:9: James 2:22; Jude 20). This is the most supernatural dimension of man's spirit because it is by faith (through grace) that a Christian receives salvation (Ephesians 2:8). Faith is also the dimension of man that allows our human spirit to receive and house the Holy Spirit. Through our faith God can sovereignly exercise His supernatural creative power to create something out of nothing as He did in Genesis or perform tangible miracles like feeding the poor and healing the sick as Christ did in the gospels.

This supernatural dimension works in man and through man to connect the realm of the supernatural and invisible with the realm of the natural and visible. **Hebrews 11:1, 3** states:

> "*[1]Now faith is the substance of things hoped for, the evidence of things not seen. [2]By faith we understand that the worlds were framed by the word of God, so that the things which are seen were not made of things which were visible.*"

The word "worlds" used in this passage is the Greek word "aiōns (αιών)" meaning age in perpetuity noting both beginning and end and agelessness. In other words, the dimension of faith reaches beyond time and bridges the eternal with the temporal. Everything that exists in the temporal was birthed from the eternal. Everything which is temporal is also dying and fading away while that which is eternal is perpetuating. Both the eternal and the temporal were created by God. Both the eternal and the temporal are components of man's triune nature. The eternal life which man has received through faith allows him to experience a reality of the eternal while in his temporal state. This is the power and the blessedness of faith.

Faith is not a fruitless belief in something, neither is it simply a positive idea or wishful thinking. Faith is the connector between divine immaterial substances and the tangible manifestation of what we believe God can do. Faith is a dimension that accomplishes the impossibilities that man cannot, and produces what is beyond man's capability. In any area that we become overly confident in our capabilities, faith and the divine ability of God become inactive. God's ability will never contend with our pride. Faith is a gift from God that we must choose to exercise.

The dimension of faith is awakened as we receive Jesus Christ as Lord and Savior and is strengthened and expanded by the hearing of the Word of God **(Romans 10:17)**. The Word of God feeds our faith, which allows us to work out our salvation. The dimension of faith is strengthened by the Word of God, prayer, fasting and work, but can be weakened by doubt, disconnection from the body of Christ and slothfulness.

CHAPTER TEN
THE DIMENSION OF PHYSICAL CYCLES

The dimension of physical cycles is often neglected in the life of the believer because we find ourselves so consumed by daily tasks and even trying to maintain a healthy spiritual life that we fail to look at our natural man (who is just as much a part of who we are as our spirit and soul). Ignoring our body's need to adhere to physical cycles such as proper sleep patterns, and proper digestion (formed by healthy eating habits) can prove costly to our Christian walk. This is a trick of the enemy. In fact, specific demons are assigned to ensure that Christians remain so heavenly minded that they do not take care of their body and become unfit to carry the gospel and accomplish the works of God. Often individuals like this are powerful men and women of God who declare the Word of God with power and authority; they preach enthusing, life changing messages, but suffer from shortness of breath because of obesity and try to incorporate infrequent breathing patterns into their preaching style. This may also apply to believers who are so overwhelmed by stress in ministry or their personal lives that they lack consistent sleep patterns or indulge in sweets late at night. These individuals may develop complications like depression, diabetes, or insomnia because they haven't sought God on how to take heed to their body's necessary physical cycles. Spiritual entities recognize our physical needs often times more than we do and the enemy uses this to his advantage.

Spiritual consecrations such as fasting and overnight prayer are beneficial to the soul and body when the consecration is chosen by God **(Isaiah 58:5)**, but should not be indulged in for vain motivations such as weight loss. Vain fasting may appear spiritual but can prove to be more fleshly and costly to one's health because it provides no spiritual virtue **(Colossians 2:23)**. Fasting should be done prayerfully under the inspiration of the Holy Spirit and it will provide discipline and virtue to body, soul and spirit. Physical cycles such as Puberty, Age, Menstruation, Menopause, Digestion, Sleep, Respiration, Circulation, Brain Activity ect. govern the productivity of our body and the process of death working in our members. From birth man is dying **(Ecclesiastes 3:1,2)**; his body produces waste, which is a sign of death; and his cells race to multiply and keep up with the thousands of cells that die daily. Man's physical cycles work to ensure that man's body works efficiently up until the appointed time when man's soul and spirit depart from his body. After death the dimension of physical cycles stops operating and the body is rendered over to rapid deterioration which in life was mediated at a slower process.

CHAPTER ELEVEN
THE DIMENSION OF HABIT

Habit is a dimension consisting of activities that are engaged unconsciously but willingly because of repetition in cause and effect (stimulus and response). Within this dimension one's original choice becomes repetitive in the response of the soul when a similar cause or stimuli is recognized. A habit is nothing more than continued behavior in light of a reoccurring event. This form of continued choice develops actions and reactions in effort to produce the same outcome.

Habit is a dimension facilitated by action, mental awareness and thought process. These components must correlate in order for a habit to be formed. Repetition in action is subject to repetition in thought processes and mental awareness. Repetition in action instills functional memory in the body. The body itself is capable of retaining physical memory. For example:

Someone who has been in a traumatic car accident may develop a habitual reaction to car rides. Now every time he gets in a car his body unconsciously begins to react to the similarity of the stimuli. He begins to sweat profusely, his heart rate accelerates and his muscles tense up.

This individual has developed an unconscious habit based on the mental state of fear which is manifested through his physical reactions. His mental awareness can also be noted in this example. Though he may not be consciously aware of his fears which stem from past experiences, his unconscious is perfectly aware of both his past experience and the similarity of his current situation. His mental awareness triggers a series of patterned thought processes. These thought processes link past emotions and memories of the traumatic event and mix them with a probability of reoccurrence based on the similarity of his current situation.

The above is an extreme example of the developmental stages within habit as they are applied to a negative situation. However the same process can be applied to less extreme, more positive examples. A habit is not necessarily a bad thing. They draw their positive or negative connotation from our reactions not from the continuity of the stimuli. Again, a habit is nothing more than a repetitive behavior in light of a similar or reoccurring event. Scripture shows us how these habits can work positively or negatively in our lives. Whatever we practice or choose consistently becomes a habit, for this reason scripture instructs us to continue in righteous things. **Romans 6:1,2** states:

> *"¹What shall we say then? Shall we continue in sin that grace may abound? ²God forbid! How shall we who died to sin live any longer in it?"*

Habitual sins can be the result of a personal pattern of sin established in the unconscious (iniquity) or a hereditary pattern of sin passed on through ones lineage (generational curse). Every person is born with an inclination to develop habitual patterns of sin. Every person, prior to salvation, has the capacity to inherit the degenerate nature of his or her forefathers. These sins plague the conscience, unconscious and subconscious mind producing degeneracy in the soul, which is manifested in habitual patterns of iniquity. However the above scriptures show us that once we accept Jesus Christ as Lord and Savior and acknowledge that in Him our sins are pardoned and removed, it is forbidden to willfully return to old habits of sin. In salvation, the grace of God has been given to us for repentance. If we can accept Christ as Savior we must also accept Him as the Way and recognize that He not only saved us from habits of sin but He set us on a new Way to develop habits of righteousness in His image and likeness. Evil, sinful habits in the believer's life are broken and replaced as we continue to practice righteousness and develop righteous habits.

CHAPTER TWELVE
THE DIMENSION OF LOVE

In the King James Version the word love appears 314 times. Love is herein described as an identity of God (1John 4:8), an expression (John 3:16), a state of being (1 Corinthians 13:4-8) and an action (Song of Solomon 8:6; Ephesians 5:25). Love is much greater and far more powerful than an emotional state or infatuation or comfort, it is like a supernatural entity that desires to cohabitate with the heart of man.

Love is an identity of God, through whom and from whom every expression of love is birthed. God is life and outside of Him nothing can live or exist, equivalently God is love and outside of Him there is no expression or experience of love. The existence and preeminence of God is what constitutes the reality of love that we experience and generate toward God and others. If man lacks the reality of the existence of the true and living God he likewise lacks the capacity to engage the dimension of love within himself as a reality. The unsaved may rightly say that they love their family, their spouse or their job. This degree of love is available simply because God exists and God's mere existence provides providential blessings for man not based on their belief but based on His existence. However, man will never experience the full reality of what love is in any of his relationships until he comes to accept who Love is. God is the source of all life so even the unsaved man has physical life not because of his belief but because of God's existence. Nevertheless the unsaved man cannot experience life more abundantly (John 10:10) until he accepts the Christ who is Life.

Within man, love is a dimension that surpasses emotions and natural ability. The dimension of love remains untapped for the unsaved because it can only be quickened by encountering the light of God (True Love, 1 John 4:8). Feelings of passion, desire and satisfaction are not to be confused with the state of being in love. In order to activate the dimension of love and assume love as a state of being one must be saved. Love as a state of being constitutes a positional grace that we receive as Christians being positioned in the body of Christ. We are *in* Love. From this posture we are able to rightly express and act on love as we are lead by the Spirit of God who cohabitates in our human spirit. This positional grace and state of being is a sign that we have passed from death to life according to **1 John 3:14**. **1 John 4:19** shows us that our ability to love is imparted unto us by the love that God sheds unto us first.

Love is not based on physical attraction or soul ties; love is formed and based in the spirit because the source of love (God) is Spirit. The mirage of love is lust. Lust is a culmination of strong desires such as covetousness, greed and misguided passions that never fully fulfill the true need of man. Man's desire to be loved and to love stems from his original need to know God. The desire to be loved is simply the compelling nature of man to be unified with what compliments and completes him.

Essentially, union with God is the only thing that can complete a man (Colossians 2:9,10; Acts 17:28). Oftentimes man looks for the representation of this union in the form of a spouse. Though a spouse cannot substitute the love of God they should compliment God's love for us. A husband or a wife should serve as a vehicle through which God can express His love to us on intimate and personal levels such as companionship. For this reason God compares the love affair between Christ and His church to that of a husband and wife (Ephesians 5:25). Scripture shows us that love is such an essential part of relationships that it always forms a covenant (whether marriage or friendship). Love in its truest form always forms a covenant, a sacred agreement recognized by God. The love between man and wife brings forth the covenant of marriage. The love between two people of agreeable and kindred spirits brings about the covenant of friendship. The love between parent and child brings forth the covenant of family. The love of the cross brought forth the covenant of salvation.

Love is the only thing in the history of man that is able to cover, overshadow and conquer sin (Proverbs 10:12; 1 Peter 4:8). Love does not exist in hell and does not exist within a hellish soul because love is and belongs to God and therefore can find no abode in what is contrary to Him. Love is a common desire of all man despite age culture or belief. Love is a necessity of the human spirit in order to fulfill the emotional and fundamental demands of the soul. Love is so fundamental to man's existence that if the presence of love were totally extracted for his internal and external environment he would cease to be. Every grace of God from the grace needed to live and breathe to the grace necessary for salvation is first rooted in God's love. If it were not for His love there would be no unmerited favor.

CHAPTER THIRTEEN
THE DIMENSION OF HATE

Hate throughout the history of man has gained a very negative connotation. However, when we look back at the origin and source of hate in human nature, we see that hate is an intended part of man's nature because of his encounter with Satan according to **Genesis 3:15**. The dimension of hate was imputed into man by God in order to establish a correct relationship between man and the devil. Hear we see that after the temptation and fall of man, not only does God describe His foreknown plan for the redemption of man in the later part of this scripture, but He also assigns man his enemy in the alpha portion. The Hebrew word for enmity used in this passage is "ayab" meaning hatred or to indentify that which is of an opposing foreign nature. Prior to the fall of man the dimension of hatred did not exist within man because he was innocent, lacking the knowledge of good and evil, being neither righteous nor corrupt, incapable of hatred or mal-emotion and possessing no adversary. In his fallen state man was now capable of choosing righteousness or corruption in light of good and evil; drawing nigh to righteousness by loving what is good; and forsaking corruption by hating what is evil.

Hatred in its right application is Godly and encouraged by God (Psalm 97:10; Ecclesiastes 3:8). We are not supposed to love everything. We are to hate satan, his works and sin, leaving no room for us to become fond of our sinful nature. What we do not hate we will not resist and will never be free from. Likewise, we must always be mindful that the sins we fail to hate, hate our God, and will begin to hinder our relationship with the Lord.

When the dimension of hatred is distorted it develops enmities and abhorrence toward God and Godly things **(Romans 8:7)**. This coercion also began in Genesis when the woman was beguiled. Originally man was created in the image and likeness of God; which would mean that sin is not just against God but it is also against the perfect nature of man. So why would man choose to assault his own soul with sin? Because "*surely* you will not die." In other words, man sins when he is first convinced that his sin is not erroneous or unrighteous; that it is lawful and or rationally justified. Eve ate of the fruit not because she wanted to sin against God, not because she wanted to ruin her perfect nature but because the thought and the deed of eating the fruit seemed justified.

Enmity against God as described in **Romans 8:7** (εχθροδ "echthros" a hostile hatred and opposition identifying an adversary) is not the manifestation of sin but the condition of the soul once perverted to look on error and lawlessness (satan) as friendly and the ordnances of God as hostile. In this distorted state man is beguiled into forgetting the enmity that was ordained for him to have with satan and all his works and is led astray in his nature to oppose the ordnances of God. The bible says in **James 1:15** *"when lust conceives, it gives birth to sin; and sin, when it is full-grown, brings forth death"*. For conception to take place there must be a womb. Lust conceives in the womb of enmity, which develops in the distorted nature of man. When the dimension of hatred is distorted it perceives God and the things of God to be hostile and puts man's nature at enmity with God.

CHAPTER FOURTEEN
THE DIMENSION OF SPOKEN WORDS

The dimension of spoken words is structured within and surrounding man. This dimension creates an invisible internal and external environment for the soul. This environment of words holds the possibility of everything that can manifest in a person's life (good or bad) depending on which words that individual chooses to accept and engage. This immaterial dimension consists of words the individual has spoken, as well as words that have been spoken concerning the individual. These words (both positive and negative) do not dissipate unless they are rebuked or confirmed by the Word of God, rather, they lurk waiting to be manifested and performed (Isaiah 55:11; Matthew 12:36).

One of the largest components of the dimension of spoken words is the Word. Genesis 1 and 2 clearly show us that all life began with the utterance of God. This principal still applies to the life of every man that has lived up to now. Though we are not directly a result of divine generation as Adam was, the life within us was predestined and spoken into existence by God (Jeremiah 1:5; Romans 8:29) and is regenerated by salvation. Most individuals fail to recognize that at birth God has already spoken concerning us. He establishes a personal declaration of who He intends for us to be. So the question is, *have you heard, accepted and engaged what God has said about you?* If not, fear not, there is a detailed outline of God's personal declaration concerning you recorded in the Word of God. The Bible is the continuous reverberation of what God has already said concerning us and His relationship to us. We must take the

Word of God and hear. The faith that we need to be who He has called us to be only comes by hearing and hearing by the Word of God **(Romans 10:17)**. We must accept what God has said and allow His Word to be converted from a part of our external environment (hearing) into a part of our internal environment (accepting and believing). After we accept what the Lord has said we can then engage the dimension of spoken words and call forth the word to produce action and manifestation.

In the lives of many people the dimension of spoken words remains fractured because they have allowed the wrong words to be introduced to their hearing and allowed these words to lurk in their external environment. As previously stated, these words do not dissipate rather they stalk the soul looking for areas of weakness that will accept them. Once we allow these words in they are engaged by our thoughts, conscious mind, unconscious mind and self-image and will manifest outwardly as we begin to declare with our mouths what our soul has accepted.

An extreme example of this can be found in the words of Jesus in **Matthew 12:34-36**:

> [34]*O generation of vipers, how can ye, being evil, speak good things? for out of the abundance of the heart the mouth speaketh.* [35]*A good man out of the good treasure of the heart bringeth forth good things: and an evil man out of the evil treasure bringeth forth evil things.* [36]*But I say unto you, That every idle word that men shall speak, they shall give account thereof in the day of judgment.*

In this passage Christ speaks to the Pharisees and addresses them as vipers. This title is given to them to allude to the lies and deception that they had accepted and voiced. This passage can be paralleled with **Isaiah 59:4-5** which states:

> [4]*None calleth for justice, nor any pleadeth for truth: they trust in vanity, and speak lies; they conceive mischief, and bring forth iniquity.* [5]*They hatch cockatrice' eggs, and weave the spider's web: he that eateth of their eggs dieth, and that which is crushed breaketh out into a viper.*

In light of this scripture we can clearly see that Christ specifically used this depiction to refer the scholarly men to a passage that would best reveal to them their error. These devote servants of God and scholars of the Word had gone astray because the dimension of spoken words was fractured. They had heaped up in their ears lies and gossip which they accepted. These words conceived within them and were venomous to their soul blinding them from the truths of who Jesus Christ was. Furthermore they engaged these untruths and acted upon them blaspheming and believing that they were justified by the lies that they held as truths. Satan is a liar and he knows it, but his aim is for you to take the lies he has spoken, accept them, and repeat them, so that the truths of Jesus Christ will never be revealed to you.

CHAPTER FIFTEEN
THE DIMENSION OF SPIRITUAL SENSES

The dimension of spiritual senses consists of our spiritual awareness; that which grants us the ability to perceive and interact with our immaterial environment. Senses such as discernment, spiritual sight and hearing the inaudible are all components of our spiritual senses. The carnal man lacks the awareness of this dimension (**1Corinthians 2:14; Hebrews 5:14**). Spiritual senses must be in order for the dichotomous nature of man to equally engage his dual natured environments. Daily we interact with both a natural and a supernatural environment. Whether we choose to embrace the reality of this or not, or whether we are cognizant of the reality of these two spheres, we still occupy and engage two spheres during our day-to-day lives. It is imperative that our five physical senses function correctly on a day-to-day basis in order for us to correctly perceive, interpret and engage our environment, it is equally important that our spiritual senses remain alert and unsheathed as we correspond with our spiritual environment.

As stated before, when man was created in the garden he was fashioned through a mediate process. Man was not called forth from one substance like plants and animals were (**Genesis 1:11,12,20-22,24-26**). **Genesis 1:26** reveals that man was created through a mediate process: his existence began in the mind of God where his purpose, authority and image were declared by God prior to his physical existence, (this was not so with the fish, the birds, the plants and the animals). Man is far more complicated than other creatures. Mankind's influence far outweighs that of any other creature. So in verse 26 God established what man's positional role would be in the earth before He placed him in his environment. **Genesis 1:27** reveals to us the second form by which man was mediated was in gender, a complete work within itself, in this verse God was not necessarily looking at Adam and Eve. The omniscience of God was gazing at the entire human race. Adam was created with Eve in him but did not have a realization of her until she was removed and presented to him (Genesis 2:18,21-23). This realization gave man the capacity for relationship.

Genesis 2:7 reveals to us the last form by which man was mediated was in substance. God formed the body of man out of the dust of the earth. God called man's physicality out of the substance of the physical environment he would have to inhabit. In doing so, man was formed perfectly conditioned to live on earth; he was equipped with the correct respiratory system to breath the kind of oxygen, nitrogen, carbon air that composes earth's atmosphere; he was created with skin to protect his internal organs from heat and abrasion; he was created erect so that he could demonstrate his positional authority over creation. Amongst other things, man's physical body was equipped with the five basic physical senses (sight, hearing, touch, smell and taste) as well as additional perceptive senses such as nociception (pain); equilibrioception (balance); proprioception and kinaesthesia (joint motion and acceleration); sense of time; thermoception (temperature differences); and magnetoception (direction). Man was completely equipped to engage his physical world.

Secondly God breathed into man's nostrils the breath of life. This portion of scripture can also be translated as such, "Jehova gave up and rendered (blew) into his face (image) the spirit of substance and life". God rendered unto man the life of his being and in doing so made him capable of interacting with his spiritual environment. The breath of life gave Adam a living spirit and a quickened soul, but it also gave us the ability to perceive and interact with spirits and the spirit realm.

Genesis 3:8 shows us that after the fall man's spirit man was injured in its self image but was still able to perceive the presence of God. This is to say that even today when God speaks both the saved (the man who has accepted the sacrifice of Christ, the Last Adam) and the unsaved (the man who continues to fall as a result of the first Adam) have the capability to hear Him, however, only the spiritual man has the capacity to rightly discern, receive and retain what he has heard (1 Corinthians 2:14). Our spirit man must be renewed daily so that our spiritual senses don't become dull (Psalm 51:10; Ephesians 4:23).

Romans 8:6 expresses to us clearly that disabling our spiritual senses debases our perception. A person who has handicapped spiritual senses is restricted to carnal perceptions and is subsequently carnally minded. While on the other hand if we give ourselves over daily to exercising our spiritual senses through a reformed spiritual mind then the rewards of life and peace belong to us. Lastly, Genesis 2:7 reveals the final phase of man's mediate creation which emerged when what was made of spiritual substance (breath of life) was introduced to what is of natural substance (body). Man became a living soul. The soul of man is what harmonizes and unifies mans physical members with his spirit.

CHAPTER SIXTEEN
THE DIMENSION OF PHYSICAL SENSES

The dimension of physical senses is imperative for our relationship with our physical environment. It is equivalent in application to discernment. Physical senses were introduced to the being of man when the physical body of man was formed. **Genesis 2:7** states, *"...and the Lord God formed man out of the dust of the earth..."*. In order for man to correctly engage his physical environment and fulfill the purpose he was designed for in Genesis 1:26 he had to have an innate relation to the substance he would inhabit and govern. Man's body could not be numb to the world around it if he was expected to govern it. God formed the body of man out of the dust of the earth. God called man's physicality out of the substance of the physical environment that he would have to inhabit. In doing so, man was formed perfectly conditioned to live in earth. He was equipped with the correct respiratory system to breath the kind of oxygen, nitrogen, carbon and air that composes earth's atmosphere. He was created with skin to protect his internal organs from heat and abrasion. He was created erect so that he could demonstrate his positional authority over creation. Amongst other things, man's physical body was equipped with the five basic physical senses (sight, hearing, touch, smell and taste) as well as additional perceptive senses such as nociception (pain); equilibrioception (balance); proprioception and kinaesthesia (joint motion and acceleration); sense of time; thermoception (temperature differences); and possibly an additional weak magnetoception (direction). Man was completely equipped to engage his physical world.

These senses also prove necessary in order for man to translate spiritually discerned things into the earth realm. For example, when the prophets Ezekiel and Isaiah beheld supernatural visions and experiences in heavenly places they later depicted to us in their writings using earthly references. These delineations, metaphors and similes are imperative in order for the revelation to be understood by men who have not yet experienced heaven in absence of the body and an earthly context. Examples of this can be seen in **Ezekiel 1:4-14amp**:

> *⁴As I looked, behold, a stormy wind came out of the north, and a great cloud with a fire enveloping it and flashing continually; a brightness was about it and out of the midst of it there seemed to glow amber metal, out of the midst of the fire. ⁵And out of the midst of it came the likeness of four living creatures [or cherubim]. And this was their appearance: they had the likeness of a man, ⁶But each one had four faces and each one had four wings. ⁷And their legs were straight legs, and the sole of their feet was like the sole of a calf's foot, and they sparkled like burnished bronze. ⁸And they had the hands of a man under their wings on their four sides. And the four of them had their faces and their wings thus: ⁹Their wings touched one another; they turned not when they went but went every one straight forward. ¹⁰As for the [ᵃ]likeness of their faces, they each had the face of a man [in front], and each had the face of a lion on the right side and the face of an ox on the left side; the four also had the face of an eagle [at the back of their heads].[4] ¹¹Such were their faces. And their wings were stretched out upward [each creature had four wings]; two wings of each one were touching the [adjacent] wing of the creatures on either side of it, and [the remaining] two wings of each creature covered its*

body. ¹²*And they went every one straight forward; wherever the spirit would go, they went, and they turned not when they went.* ¹³*In the midst of the living creatures there was what looked like burning coals of fire, like torches moving to and fro among the living creatures; the fire was bright and out of the fire went forth lightning.* ¹⁴*And the living creatures darted back and forth like a flash of lightning.*

This artistic depiction uses the physical sense of sight as a channel to illuminate revelation concerning a greater vision that the author experienced. Verses 4-14 focus on the subject of the angelic beings surrounding God's presence, which give deeper insight concerning the judgment of God throughout time. The fiery wind rising out of the north with amber colored radiance was emblematic of the divine judgment that rose out of the north from Babylon in 588-586 BC. The four living creatures addressed in this passage possessing the numeric properties of four symbolizes God's sovereign authority over the four corners of the earth and the posture of the angels implies their readiness to execute God's command everywhere. The embellished language used to illustrate their fierce appearance also reveals their superiority over things of the earth and their heavenly origin. Most intriguing is the illustration of the countenance of the faces of each creature. It is noteworthy that the description of the faces of the four living creatures can also be interpreted as symbolic of "the four portraits of Jesus" as given in the four Gospels. Matthew represents our Lord as the King (the lion), Mark portrays Him as the Servant (the ox), Luke emphasizes His humanity (man) and John proclaims especially His deity (the eagle).

The above example shows us how the Lord uses our physical sense of sight to interpret spiritual revelation. The interpretation provides man with a multidimensional understanding of the greater knowledge that God is conveying to him. One should not overly indulge in the dimension of physical senses as to produce lust, but as we pursue a deeper understanding of the things of God we should be aware that physical senses in line with spiritual senses can be used as a tool to open our perception and understanding of scripture.

CHAPTER SEVENTEEN
THE DIMENSION OF THE CONSCIENCE MIND

The conscience mind is defined by the Dorland's Medical Dictionary as "an inner moral sense that distinguishes right acts from wrong. Conscience is not always an adequate justification for action," and is the dimension where man deliberates his opinion of good and evil as a result of what he's perceived through his conscious, unconscious and subconscious. The dimension of conscience requires the full development of the conscious, which is the "state of having awareness of oneself and of one's acts and surroundings; a state of alertness or awareness characterized by response to external stimuli. The part of the mind that is constantly within awareness, one of the systems of Freud's topographic model of the mind" (Dorland's Medical Dictionary).

The dimension of the conscience mind evolved in man directly after the fall of Adam and Eve hereafter mankind entered the dispensation of conscience. When the dispensation of conscience was implemented man received the knowledge of good and evil and this knowledge constructed within his soul the capacity for choice. Now man is capable of choosing to take on the identity of righteousness or corruption. Mankind as a whole was given the power to judge his own actions and disposition within the context of good and evil. Man was now capable of sin because his choices were based on the judgments of a conscience mind and not instinct. The Bible does not record that Adam sinned, but simply that he fell from his perfect, innocent state. However, Cain's act of murder was a sin because he made a choice in light of a conscience mind (Genesis 4:6,7). This shows us that sin is not a direct result of choice alone, rather it is a result of the choices we make as a result of misguided judgments made by our conscience mind.

The conscience mind in man is not an inherent attribute rather it is an inevitable development that a child acquires as he transitions from childhood to adolescence. **Proverbs 22:6** shows us the importance of exampling to a child the differences between good and evil so that this impression may remain with him as he develops his personal set of morals after reaching adolescence.

After adolescence the individual deciphers and identifies within his conscience mind two sets of moral values, these sets of moral values determine what the individual interprets as good and evil. The first set of moral values is social. Social morals are developed through parental instruction, observation and adherence to the popular standards of good and evil commonly accepted by ones social environment, these include: social norms, cultural expectations, religion, family and education. The second set of moral values is personal, which is developed through experience, spirituality and personal interpretation of our external environment.

CHAPTER EIGHTEEN
THE DIMENSION OF THE UNCONSCIOUS

The unconscious is separate from the conscious and subconscious but is available and active during consciousness, reacting apart from the will. The unconscious is very similar to a sponge hidden in the deep recesses of our mind. Like a sponge, the unconscious retains memory, experience and habits that have been developed over time. Throughout the day our unconscious is fed by what we receive through our senses. The unconscious does not decipher this information and respond based on the choice of our will, rather it leaks out responses, behaviors and communications while our conscience mind is unaware. The unconscious is responsible for thoughts, phobias, desires and perceptions that we engage without the consent of our conscience mind.

In actuality the conscious mind is hundreds of milliseconds behind the unconscious processes. What the unconscious mind will perceive and receive as truth may take the conscious mind minutes to years to effectively process. The unconscious is a wonderful mechanism that God divided in the mind of man. Because of the unconscious, experiences, truths and realities that may very well overwhelm our conscious mind (producing insanity) can be received by the unconscious and slowly fed to the conscious mind for further processing. For example:

An individual who witnesses the death of a loved one may go into shock (seeming emotionless and unresponsive to the reality of the situation) because he is unable to process consciously the emotions and reality of the situation. Years later this individual may find a trinket that reminds them of the individual and the emotions and information that they did not deal with in the past may begin to slowly arise and flood the conscious mind.

This individual can now process mourning slowly without being overwhelmed. This relationship and process between the unconscious and the conscious is called repression and emergence. Repression and emergence is a psychological mechanism given by God to assist man with dealing with even larger truths.

When the bible speaks of divine visions being given to men it is often referring to a spiritual insight that was ministered to them. These visions were usually so overwhelming that they could not be interpreted with human reasoning. A messenger of God was used to covey the understanding of the message to the conscious mind and translate the truths which the unconscious had already received **(Daniel 7:1-14,15).**

.

CHAPTER NINETEEN
THE DIMENSION OF THE SUBCONSCIOUS

The subconscious dimension incorporates déjà vu, dreams and day dreams. Like the unconscious the subconscious is partially aware during consciousness and is able to receive and perceive stimuli. Unlike the unconscious the subconscious is not expressed during consciousness. During consciousness the subconscious often attracts spiritual things and retains a log of our unconscious interactions. Those with high levels of discernment and spiritual awareness also have high levels of activity in there subconscious. The subconscious relates to the physical realm and the spiritual realm as equal realities, expressing spiritual things as physical beings. The subconscious mind does not express things according to their literal value but rather conveys their symbolic meaning in order to relate a message **(Daniel 2:1; Joel 2:28; Acts 2:17)**.

When interpreting the expressions of the subconscious the colors, sizes, shapes, sounds, and smells of everything represented present abstract meanings and must be considered in their symbolic content in order to determine the overall meaning. While this dimension does deal with information abstractly it uses symbols to relate the true value of the information to the person. The subconscious assigns symbols that are personally meaningful so that we can extract the meaning of the overall message having evaluated each symbol according to their value. For example, a small red frog in my dream may represent a small fear in my life that could be dangerous to me. We can draw this interpretation if we knew that I had a small fear of frogs in real life and that I commonly understood the color red to be a warning sign. Nevertheless, this same symbol appearing in someone else's dream may mean a small friendship is coming because that individual culturally understands frogs to be a symbol of friendship and the color red to be a symbol of love. The subconscious only has the power to generate symbols off of what we have already received, or understood.

In interpreting what our subconscious illustrates to us we must also take into consideration the source of the underline message. The subconscious like the unconscious receives stimuli from our environment and the conscious mind processes this information later. The subconscious has the ability to receive from God, from our own thoughts, or from demonic projections. Not all dreams come from God and not all nightmares come from satan, sometimes the source of our subconscious expression comes from us. Unresolved thoughts that we wrestle with throughout the day or late night eating can play tricks on our subconscious mind **(Ecclesiastes 5:3)**. The enemy knows our weaknesses and our strengths and understands that often times he cannot get to us while we are conscious. So, he waits and plays on our fears and insecurities through our subconscious. Even bad dreams, which are afflicted unto a man by the devil, may be allowed by God in order to get His message across **(Daniel 2)**. Dreams and subconscious expressions that are from God are easily interpreted through prayer, godly council and the Word of God.

CHAPTER TWENTY
THE DIMENSION OF HEALTH

When we speak of the dimension of health we are to include physical, mental, emotional and spiritual health. The health of the whole man is contingent upon the health of both our physical and spiritual parts according to **3 John 1:2**, *"Beloved, I wish above all things that thou mayest prosper and be in health, even as thy soul prospereth."* This scripture shows us that there can be no prosperity where health does not prevail. Sickness and degeneracies in our physical and spiritual body cannot produce prosperity for the whole man. The dimension of health is essential because it fortifies and provides strength for the other twenty-six plus dimensions.

The Merriam Webster Dictionary defines health as "the condition of being sound in body, mind, or spirit; especially: freedom from physical disease or pain". Health implies balance. Health increases in a man when he is able to take care of his members by supplying them with the necessary sustenance and exercise so that his members can operate according to their natural order. The physical body requires a balanced diet, proper rest and adequate exercise in order to function in good health. The spiritual body requires the Word of God, faith and an adequate relationship with God in order to function in good health. The soul of man has a twofold need, requiring love and good relationship to produce emotional health, and education and self-confidence to produce intellectual health.

In a Christian's life health is increased as we allow ourselves to be strengthened by the vigor of the life in Christ.

In every man's life health is weakened by immorality and sin. Immorality and sin produces degeneracy and diseases within our soul, which are expressed through our physical bodies. Often times (but not every time) the ailments that rid our body are a result of the diseases that infect our souls **(Psalm 38:3; Isaiah 1:6)**. Man's fall into sin produced disease and pestilence in the world. Prior to this, sickness did not exist in the garden. Sickness is also recorded in the Bible as being attributed to individuals who were demon possessed or oppressed **(Matthew 4:24; 8:16; Luke 6:17,18)**. Sickness is not always a sign of just bad health; it may be a sign of an infected soul. In either case, weather sickness is introduced to the body as a result of sin, demonic influence or natural cause; the elixir to all sickness is Christ. In every instance of illness recorded in the Gospels health was restored to the person when their illness was confronted by Christ.

Christ has the remedy to restore the dimension of health within all men whether their illness is spiritual or natural (or whether the cause of their sickness is natural or supernatural). The remedy for sickness in the soul as a result of sin is found in the deliverance power of Christ Jesus. The remedy for sickness caused as a result of demonic possession and oppression is found in the authority of the name of Jesus. The remedy for sickness in the body is found in the miracle working power of God. Many illnesses of the natural body can be healed by medicine but what medicine cannot heal Christ can **(Luke 4:18)**. Health is essential in the life of the believer in order to fulfill purpose and be effective in our works for the kingdom of God. As human beings we are extremely frail creatures. It is a miracle by the grace of God every time God uses us frail humans to do His work. A healthy spirit, soul and body are essential to a believer who desires to endure the weight of carrying out the purposes of God in the earth. Our health is not to be considered secondary to the work of God. Rather it should be considered a part of our necessary equipping before engaging the work of the Lord. An athlete requires a healthy body to perform his purpose. A philosopher needs a healthy mind in order to enlighten and expand his thoughts. Likewise, a Christian requires a healthy spirit, soul and body in order to effectively accomplish God's purpose with the limited time he is allotted. Our life in the earth is too short to spend days, months and years ill and handicapped from the work of the Lord.

CHAPTER TWENTY-ONE
THE DIMENSION OF MEMORY

Memory is the ability to store, retain and recall information. Memory is both a physical function of the brain and a spiritual function of the mind. Memory stored in the brain is supported by the prefrontal lobe, the parietal lobe and the hippocampus. Memory as a component of the mind is stored in the soul of man as is proven by scripture in **Luke 16:19-28**. The two characters in this passage were able to remember and identify one another in absence of their natural bodies implying that memory goes deeper then the capability of the physical brain. Memory is spiritual.

Our natural ability to retain memory is restricted and memories can be altered if the brain undergoes extreme changes such as stress, injury or Alzheimer. As a result of these changes one may begin to alter their memory unknowingly. Likewise, memory as a spiritual component of the mind is susceptible to the changes in the dimension of experience, emotions, self-image and perception. It is human nature to alter our recollection of the past to fit our current perception of ourselves and the world around us. Memory is not concrete history it is a *personal* recount of a past event but if the element of *personhood* changes in any sense the memory may also be altered.

In **Philippians 3:13** Paul states:

> *"Brethren, I count not myself to have apprehended: but this one thing I do, forgetting those things which are behind, and reaching forth unto those things which are before".*

Paul at this time had altered his personhood from Saul of Tarsus to Paul the Apostle of Jesus Christ and found it necessary to cast off his memory of his dead nature (as God did) in order to acquire what the Lord had for him. Two truths concerning Christian memory are presented here: the first being that we must forget our sins and our dead lives as God did and secondly that we must do so in order to acquire what God has for us in our new nature.

Man is like God in the dimension of memory because he was given the ability to choose, at liberty, to retain or forget information. The Bible tells us in **Hebrew 8:12; 10:17** that God so loathes the idea of our sins and the thought of our old sinful identity that he chooses to forget it **(Psalm 103:12; Micah 7:19)**. God in no way desires that our old identity be associated with our new nature, not even in thought. Therefore, as we take on the image of Christ Jesus we take on His attributes as well choosing to forget those things, which were formerly a part of our identity. Nothing can be poured into a full vessel. In order for us to attain the new things that God offers us in Christ Jesus we must commit ourselves to forgetting old things and remembering the new identity God declared of us in scripture **(Romans 8:29)**.

The only form of memory that is not susceptible to such changes is "ischus" a Greek word which refers to the ability to have supernatural memory of the Word of God. The Word of God is unchanging and ischus allows the witness of the Holy Ghost to reside in our memory so that we retain an unchanging memory of God's unchanging Word. By ischus God not only imparts new truths into our lives, he commits them to our memory so that we retain an unfailing identity in Christ **(Acts 11:16; Lamentations 3:20;)**.

CHAPTER TWENTY-TWO
THE DIMENSION OF EXPERIENCE

The dimension of experience is a hard dimension of man, the structure of this dimension is less morphic and more solid. What happened happened, and in this dimension past knowledge and reflexes are added to habits and memory **(Luke 24:14; Philippians 1:12)**. Experience is retained in the body as motor memory, physical scars and apart of our physical development and growth. Experience affects our soul the most. What we draw from our experiences forms our opinions, biases, perceptions ect. While our body retains physical memory of our physical experiences and our spirit retains the memory of our spiritual experiences the soul retains both physical and spiritual experiences. Man does not have the power to alter this dimension at all though he does have a choice as to how much he draws from it.

In life some experiences are drastic (whether good or bad) and leave lasting impressions and indentations on our personality and perspective. When this happens we have the choice to either embrace the experience, learn from it, and continue to move on with our lives, or we may halt our personal development by centralizing our lives around that experience. When one chooses to centralize all their opinions, actions and essentially their personality around a single experience that individual cripples their development and hinders the potential for personal growth. For example:

Say a young girl in third grade becomes best friends with someone and she bonds with this person emotionally (building trust and love), intellectually (sharing common likes and dislikes), and socially (being in the same class and age bracket), but their relationship ends when one has to move away. This young girl was never taught how to form new relationships and never makes new friends. This child grows up to be a successful young woman who lacks social skills and is subsequently isolated from people in general.

What has happened here is in the area of relationship the young ladies growth was hindered because she was unable to progress from one experience to the next. In this instance her capacity to experience new relationships and build new bonds was crippled. Whenever an individual secludes one experience and establishes that experience as the cap of all future encounters they leave no room for God to add to their lives. Life includes experiences, but one experience is not all inclusive of the measure and extent of what God intends for us.

Another good example of progression (from experience to experience) adding to the development of an individual can be found when we look at the life of King David. This mighty man of valor began as a shepherd, conquering lions and bears, progressed to being a soldier who slayed a giant, a general who triumphed over tens of thousands and a king who built an empire and established a throne in the name of the Lord. Each of David's experiences added to his development progressively. The dimension of experience is not intended to be stagnant and limited by the past, but progressive.

CHAPTER TWENTY-THREE
THE DIMENSION OF THE DEGENERATE MAN

The dimension of the degenerate man can be defined as the active personality and life style of the unbeliever. The degenerate man is the expression of the fallen nature of Adam existing in the life of everyman who is devoid of Christ. Prior to salvation this is the identity of every human in the earth young or old, male and female, despite race or creed (Psalm 51:5). The degenerate man is the full potential of each human's Adamic identity; in which each man's sinful identity is equally corrupt but personally different. One man's Adamic identity may be more susceptible to the sin of homosexuality while the other is to lying.

This dimension has the capability of having a standard of moral good best exampled by unsaved humanitarians. The standard of morality within this dimension does not exist as a result of being aware of God's standards rather it is a result of general conscience in light of a man made definition of good and evil. Having knowledge of good and evil and choosing what is good is worth nothing if the definition of good and evil is manmade and not God conscious. A humanly good man is not the same as a saved man. Even the good deeds of the degenerate man will pass away and be counted as nothing. But the redeemed man accomplishes his works through Christ, working out the everlasting purposes of God in the earth.

The dimension of the degenerate man is disclosed and sealed in a believer's life according to **2 Corinthians 5:17** which states:

"Therefore if any man be in Christ, he is a new creature: old things are passed away; behold, all things are become new."

The theantric action of Christ puts to death our old man through the crucifixion and burial of Jesus Christ and raises us up as new men reborn in our spirit through the resurrection of Christ Jesus. We are reborn with a new capacity, a new conscience and a new identity in Christ and can only access the old man by choice. The new man reacts out of conviction in light of the moral standard of God, while the degenerate man has no convictions.

A choice to attempt to resurrect the old man is a blatant sign of under appreciation of the grace of God, which departed us from that identity. The degenerate man is dead. Therefore, nothing about our old identity has the power to produce life. Dead things stink, rot and bring disease to living things. Likewise, if we try to adhere to the patterns and behaviors of our old identity and bring those dead things into our new Christian identity we may find ourselves spiritually sick and sickening to God **(Revelation 3:16)**. The degenerate man and the redeemed man cannot coexist one must be put to the slaughter. **(Romans 6:6; Ephesians 4:22; Colossians 3:9).**

CHAPTER TWENTY-FOUR
THE DIMENSION OF THE REDEEMED MAN

The redeemed man is the personality and life of the believer. It is the whole reformation of man after he accepts Christ Jesus. The redeemed man is not an improvement to the degenerate man; rather the redeemed man is altogether a new creation possessing a new identity in Christ. The redeemed man has power over the old man **(Ephesians 2:24)** and is empowered by the life of Christ to live in righteousness. This is not to say that in our redeemed state that we do not sin and make error because all men fall short of God's glory **(Romans 3:23)**. Nevertheless, this is to say that that the redeemed man has been empowered with conviction and repentance to turn from his wicked ways, while the degenerate man will never see his errors because the light of the Gospel does not shine on him. The degenerate man cannot be improved to produce salvation. He must be killed and the life of Christ that we receive through salvation generates within us a new life and a new identity. Through the redeemed man we house and express the image of Christ **(Colossians 3:10)**.

Though we are accepted into one body (the church, body of Christ) and are all filled with the same Holy Spirit we all receive a personal identity in Christ. That is to say, there are no clones in God each Christian has an individually unique identity as a redeemed man. For this reason some Christians personify distinctly the meekness of Christ through their new identity while others personify distinctly the mercy of Christ. Our redeemed identity is as personal as our individuality yet it is that binding factor that unites the whole man with God and other believers **(Ephesians 2:15)**. The redeemed man gives us one accord with believers past and present, here and there. The redeemed man is equipped with supernatural communication with God in the form of prayer, intersession, praise and worship. Finally, the redeemed man is the only kind of human that will be accepted into heaven. Man will not gain entrance into heaven because of morality, philosophy or enlightenment; he will be permitted into heaven because he has the substance of heaven already in him (the image of Christ).

CHAPTER TWENTY-FIVE
THE DIMENSION OF SELF-IMAGE

The dimension of self-image is developed based on internal and external opinions. The self-image that we have of ourselves can be compared to a mirror that examines us as a whole and presents before us an image of who we perceive ourselves to be (Proverbs 27:19). The image we formulate of ourselves develops as a result of the self-awareness process. From birth we begin this process. As children we begin by identifying who we are by association. We look at other humans around us and based on likeness we determine a reality of gender, a positional identity in our family, and a realization of age and maturity. In adolescence, we refine our definition of self by perceiving culture, physical traits and exploring our own personality. As we enter adulthood we refine our definition of self, considering our economic status, skill, education, social status, religion and likelihood of advancement.

Our self-image is ever evolving as we continue to develop and change our identity and what we identify ourselves with. When we consider the opinions of others and formulate our opinion of self we construct truths about who we are. However, usually when these truths are confronted by God's opinion of us we realize how far off our subjective opinions are. In fact, God always formulates a more positive and objective opinion of who we are (Jeremiah 29:11). The best way to construct a healthy self-image is to forsake all other opinions and adhere to what God has said concerning us as outlined in scripture.

CHAPTER TWENTY-SIX
THE DIMENSION OF ACTION

Action is a dimension which operates in the physical as well as the spiritual realm. Both our physical and spiritual environments are engaged in continuous action and events. Likewise, both our physical and spiritual man is continuously acting upon our intensions (both conscious and subconscious) within these two spheres **(Matthew 16:27; John 6:28, 14:12)**. A form of spiritual action includes planning because this is the motion of thought which precedes the execution of intent. Spoken words are another form of spiritual action because these words put into motion invisible works prior to the manifestation of what was said. This is well exampled when we look at the ministry of John the Baptist. **Mark 1:1-8** and **Matthew 3:1-12** shows us that John the Baptist committed himself to preaching repentance for the remission of sin because the kingdom of heaven was at hand. His spiritual action of preaching prepared the people and the region spiritually so that they could receive the manifestation of their repentance and the source of their remission of sin when He appeared.

The Bible also shows us that both spiritual action and physical works must accompany faith. **James 2:26** declares, *"for as the body without the spirit is dead, so faith without works is dead also."* What we believe God for cannot be accomplished by our faith if it is not accompanied by physical and spiritual action. We must pray and declare with our mouths what we have faith for and set the spiritual realm into action, but we must also put forth efforts of faith with our hands in order to see faith accomplish.

Faith requires bodily action. By faith we can believe that God will provide us with a multimillion-dollar business (and He can), but if we don't agree with our faith by putting forth the action of creating the paper work, building an idea, and talking to people, then we give our faith nothing to work with. We must remember that our physical actions speak to our natural and spiritual audience. The worst thing would be for us to allow our mouths to speak of our faith in God while our actions (or failure to act) speak of doubt.

CHAPTER TWENTY-SEVEN
THE DIMENSION OF THE RELATIONSHIP

The most unique and complex dimension of man is the dimension of relationship in which the twenty-seven dimensions of one human being is engrafted and enmeshed into that of another person. There are over 6.8 billion people in the earth and not a single human being in the earth is isolated in his existence. Human life in general was created social so that regardless of what degree or to what extreme every man's life affects another; if this was not so than the fall of Adam would have been isolated from the rest of mankind. Every man on earth has a general relation to the rest of the human race.

When we speak more personally of the relationships of the individual, we see that the dimension of relationship is a unique capacity within each individual. The dimension of relationship attracts what is most like it. We do not reflect our company; our company reflects the deepest part of who we are. The relationships we form reveal to us what truly resides in the other twenty-six dimensions of our being and in doing so they show us whether our identity is found in Christ or in the world (1 John 3:14; 2:15). The strongest connection between a person and the world is not their connection to materialistic things but their connection to worldly people (Romans 12:2).

Relationships are formed in the spirit realm first where the soul recognizes agreement, common ground, and acceptance and is willing to mesh with another soul. In 1 Samuel 18:1,3 we read that the heart of David was knit with the heart of Jonathan. The word for knit used here is "Qashar" meaning to bring into covenant, to join together gird and strengthen. This concept of relationship applies to friendship, family, marriage and salvation.

Originally, all man is born alienated from God (Colossians 1:2,19). Sin formed alienation in the dimension of relationship in every man since the fall of Adam (Genesis 3:9-12 vs. 2:23; Colossians 1:21,22). Our alienation from God alienated us from one another and from knowing ourselves. This alienation created a deformity in man because man was not only created to be a social being but a unified being, being one with God, himself and his fellow man. Outside of God man's individual nature is in disarray giving him no access to the depth of his own inner nature, making it impossible to establish depth relationships with others. Because he is detached from his identity he cannot invite anyone in to meet the man he does not know.

Christ repaired this dimension between man and God (John 17:11), between man and others (Galatians 3:28; Ephesians 2:15,16) and between man and himself (Ephesians 4: 4-6). Our acceptance into the body of Christ removes the alienation and restores harmony in the dimension of relationship. It takes time for us to develop a relationship with God and likewise it takes time for us to develop a relationship with others and even with ourselves. Be patient. The dimension of relationship is so delicate that if we try to force a connection that is not naturally built over time, we can in turn assault the balance of our internal nature. Every relationship is built on some level of sharing and receiving... but even this must be done carefully. Christ Himself never forced Himself on anyone but entreats them to accept him, fellowship with him, and build a relationship with him (Revelation 3:20).

  As we build connections in the dimension of relationship we are actually linking ourselves to the soul of another person. While a shallow relationship may be secluded to a few laughs here and there, other relationships root individuals deep into our love, our hurt, our memories, ect. We must be careful who we allow into the sacred corridors of our being. Permitting access to a stranger can be like inviting a cunning thief to invade the treasury of your heart. The wisest way to build a relationship is with the joint consultation of the Holy Spirit. In other words, if you have a relationship that you do not feel comfortable with the Lord looking in on... maybe that's not a relationship you should have. It is foolish to try to hide our relationships from an omniscient God. It is even more foolish to try to withdraw from our relationship with God to pursue a relationship where He is not invited.

CLOSING SUMMARY

Man was created in the image and likeness of God but from his fallen state man must be reborn into the image and likeness of Jesus Christ. There are over twenty-seven dimensions of man all of which remain naked before God in need of His life changing power. The psalmist asked in **Psalm 8:4,5** *"What is man that You are mindful of him?..."* the simple answer is that man is a wonderful creation of God, complicated and fearfully and wonderfully made, but a Christian is a son of God reborn into the image and likeness of Jesus Christ the first born of many brethren. Christ thought it not robbery to be equal with God but came in the form of a servant so that man could be reconciled unto God. God Himself took on the form of man so that man could take on the image and character of Christ and become one in Christ Jesus even as He and the Father are one **(John 17:21).**

The human existence is multi-dimensional, but the Word of God is perfectly designed to minister to and engage the whole person. The Word of God was created to minister to man in every dimension of his existence. While Christ's deity was the power behind the action of salvation, His humanity made it so that salvation was available for the whole man in every dimension. Jesus Christ was a sacrifice and is a Savior who was perfect in every dimension of His humanity.

> *"Therefore He is able to save to the uttermost those who come to God through Him, since He [Christ in his glorified state] always lives to make intercession for them"* **Hebrews 7:25.**

As we continue in our Christian walk we must allow the Spirit of God to arouse the nature of Christ in our lives, transfiguring each dimension of our being. Through this daily transformation by the Spirit and the Word of God we fearfully work out our salvation so that the whole man might be saved spirit, soul and body **(Philippians 2:12; 1 Thessalonians 5:23)**. He that began a good work in us shall complete it until the day of Jesus Christ. We must yield to the transforming power of God and allow the light of His Spirit to search our inward man, examine every dimension, and make us whole, as we are reformed daily into the image and likeness of Christ Jesus.

SPECIAL THANKS

I would like to extend my deepest gratitude to my mentor and spiritual father Apostle Brian Keith Sinclair, Ph.D. Founder of Triumphant World Outreach and, Dean and Chancellor of Tabernacle Bible College & Seminary *New England.* Throughout the years your sermons have inspired me, your wisdom has counseled me, and your instruction has taught me the love of God and the immutable truth of His word. I pray this book will bless others the way your life has been a blessing to me.

Thank You